"...LISTEN To Me!"

Life Lessons
from 45
Years of
Pouring
Concrete

John R. Peretto

Dedication

To Natalie Gianulias Peretto,
my Greek Wife.
You saved me and brought me back to life.

Acknowledgments

- God - The whole source of everything
- My wife Natalie Gianulias Peretto
- My deceased wife Suzanne Corona-Marie Perron Peretto
- Paul and Valerie White
- Rudy and Connie Peretto
- Rudy and Matt Peretto
- Robin Peretto
- Uncle "Wee-wee" Hank MacKenzie
- My co-workers: John Coffey, Jim Hickey, Tom Rainford, Indian Joe, and Stewart Ayres
- Russ Word
- A-Bade
- My grandchildren: Dominic, Allie, Sierra, and Alex
- Dr. David Begert
- All my cousins (and there are a lot of them)
- LeRue Press for your patience and professionalism

Table of Contents

JOHN PERETTO

"I'm just an ordinary
working man."

INTRODUCTION

How I learned the important things I'm sharing with you

I was a public school student who was forced to go to a private school.

I acted up and got into trouble all the time; but somehow, the nuns didn't kick me out and I graduated.

After the military and college, my parents helped me get a job as an apprentice draftsman with the best company in town. I got a credit card, company car, and got to sit at a desk in a back office. I wore dress pants and nice shoes, and traced drawings 8 hours a day. My parents were happy because I had a job I could do for 30 years.

Two days later I quit and joined the Laborers' Union.

That night at dinner, with all my family gathered around the table, my police officer dad asked me how my new office job was going. When I told him I'd quit to become a union laborer, he coughed so hard that the meatball he had just put in his mouth popped out and hit my brother Rudy in the head.

"You went to college!" he roared. "You could have a nice steady job as a cop or a draftsman, and you want to just be a LABORER?

"Damn right, Dad," I responded. "Not JUST a laborer...a UNION laborer. That's what I want to be."

I eventually ended up in the Cement Masons Union, making more than both my parents put together. I bought my first house at 20, and sent my parents on an all-expenses paid trip to Italy.

I was blessed by God with 45 years of a full career with a major construction company, and an even fuller life.

Why should you listen to what I'm sharing in this book?

Because I'm a good example of a God-fearing American - someone who grew up mostly on my own, had some big challenges and made a million mistakes, but I fought through ALL of them, and built myself a wonderful life.

But this little book is not about ME.

It's about what I've LEARNED and proven the hard way.

It's my thoughts, opinions, and advice about a wide range of important issues that can help YOU have a wonderful life, also.

I believe that if you think about the lessons in this book - and apply them - you'll start to feel the same way about YOUR life, that I feel about my OWN:

"It doesn't get much better than this!"

CHOOSING A CAREER...

Chapter ONE

DON'T choose a job because of how much it pays or what your title is.
Pick a job that you LIKE.

I picked a career that I knew I would be happy doing the rest of my life...and I was! People criticized my choice, but I didn't listen, and it worked out great.

Pick something you would really LIKE to do, regardless of the pay or status, or what other people think about it. THEN...dive into it and do the best possible job you can.

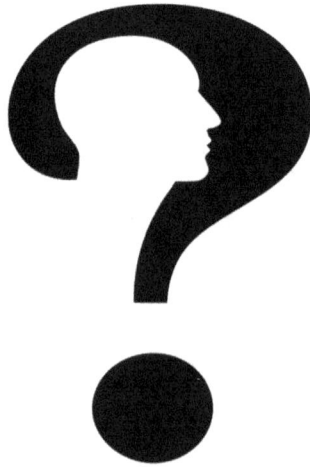

CHANGING
YOUR LIFE

Chapter TWO

If I could re-live my life, I'd do EVERYTHING exactly the same.

- Don't regret ANYTHING. It won't change what happened, and just wastes the REST of your life.
- Learn from your mistakes.
- Fix whatever you screwed up, when possible...and move on.

HOW TO BE HAPPY

Chapter THREE

It's up to YOU
to make yourself happy.

- Nobody else and NOTHING else can make you happy.
- Not money - Not a fancy job. Not a great mate, not ANYTHING else.
- Happiness comes from WITHIN you.
- Fight every day to stay grateful for all the blessings in your life.

DRUGS & ALCOHOL

Chapter FOUR

I've never believed in drugs at all. I can't stand them.

Alcohol can be just as bad, but if God drank wine, I can drink it.

You have to watch out for the dependency.

Everyone wants to stay healthy, but some people have terrible things happen to them that are not their fault, like sickness and disease. That's why people who ARE blessed with good health, and then screw it up themselves with drugs or too much alcohol, are stupid and ungrateful SOB's. Be grateful for the health God gave you, and don't abuse it.

Drug rehabs are mostly a farce, but it depends on the person. They CAN work, but most addicts are just forced to go to them. As soon as they get out, they start doing the same thing again.

Stay out of the bars.
Have the courage to deal with reality.

**You're smart enough and
strong enough to deal
with whatever your problems are.**

3 STEPS FOR SOLVING
TOUGH PROBLEMS

Chapter FIVE

- **Don't read too much into the problems.**
- **The steps we need to take are simple, if you really think about it.**
- **You KNOW the difference between good and bad, and the steps you need to take.**

Take those steps TODAY.

In my high school yearbook, the quote I chose for myself was, *"Life is tough, but I shall conquer."*

In my life, I did just that; and with the help of God, all my tough problems have been solved.

You can do it too.

MY #1 QUESTION
FOR GOD

Chapter SIX

I would ask God, "Why did you give us free will? All we're doing is screwing things up."

NO one - especially politicians, should have free-will. We can't handle it. Take responsibility for what you do, especially with sex. It's someone's life.

MONEY

Chapter SEVEN

There is no reason in HELL why anyone today doesn't have enough money.

- The only reason people don't have money is because they aren't willing to work hard enough to have it.
- Money governs almost everyone in the world...but not ME.
- If you're smart, you won't let it govern YOU, either.

(And make sure you always give some to others.)

"Remember:

There is Right and Wrong.
There is NOTHING in-between."

Chapter EIGHT

THREE OF THE MOST IMPORTANT THINGS TO KNOW

- **There is a God.**
  I believe in Him - and if you're smart, you will, too.
- **Most of the people in the world today are goofy.**
  You have to find a way to deal with them.
- **Obey Jesus: "Love your neighbor as yourself."**
  If EVERYONE did that, there would be no crime - no problems.

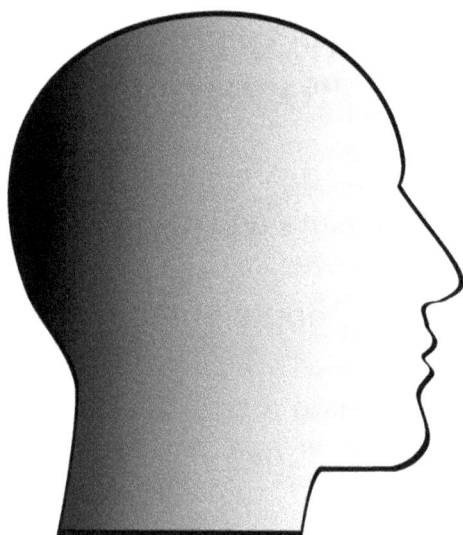

RACE

Chapter NINE

This race shit makes me sick!

Things have changed.

Races staying separated is not the big deal it was in my parents' day.

Race problems today are NOT about skin color. They're about cultural differences.

Like ANY honest parent, I'd probably prefer my children to marry someone of their own race and culture because it would be easier for them.

But if they really loved someone who's different from them, it would be no big deal.

People use their own race, or blame other races as a leverage stick to get what they want.

Blacks and Whites have had it the easiest.

Asians and Latinos have had to work the hardest.

Can you imagine how great it would be if all the races got together and worked together on things that really mattered?

Race doesn't tell if one color is better or worse than another.

STATISTICS tell who is doing better and who is doing worse.

If any race doesn't like what other races are blaming them for...they need to quit blaming it on "racism," look at their statistics, and work to change THEM.

ABORTION

Chapter TEN

You have the right to screw up your OWN life. You DON'T have the right to take someone else's.

Abortion is no different than going out and killing someone, because you're killing a baby. With more than 15 kinds of birth control, how do you ACCIDENTALLY get pregnant?

I don't buy the excuses.

PARENTING

Chapter ELEVEN

The best way to ruin your kids is to give them everything they want - at any time they want it.

The most important thing a parent can teach their child is morality. How else will a child learn what is Good and what is Bad? When you bring a child into the world, the PARENTS' job is to set an example.

You have to teach your children how to live good, clean, responsible lives. You must set a good example in EVERYTHING you do, including: mowing your lawn, washing your car, not using cuss words, turning off the junk on TV, and so on.

HOW DO YOU DISCIPLINE KIDS WHO WON'T OBEY THEIR PARENTS?

Take an active interest in them, and watch them closely. If a kid is really bad - you have to put MORE time into them. But sometimes, kids STILL decide they're going to do things THEIR way and not listen to anyone, (like I did many times).

When they do that, they usually get a consequence that hurts them, and THEN they learn.

It's too bad, and it doesn't HAVE to be that way; but that's how most of us learn. It's the time and effort parents commit to their kids that makes the difference.

> *...forgive* one another, even as God for Christ's sake has forgiven you. (St. Paul)

FORGIVENESS

Chapter TWELVE

Forgive EVERYTHING and EVERYONE.

There was a long time in my life when I would never forgive things.

As I got older, and experienced terrible things - like my wife and friends dying, it made me understand that holding a grudge is no good.

It's a sickness inside YOU that eats at YOU.

Now, I forgive everything.
So should you.

A SUCCESSFUL LIFE

Chapter THIRTEEN

WHAT IS A SUCCESSFUL LIFE?

A successful life is getting up happy and grateful every day and going to bed happy and grateful every night.

People think success is having lots of money and big jobs.
It's NOT.
Success is having - and appreciating the simple things.

POURING CONCRETE

Chapter FOURTEEN

Pouring concrete made me a better man and a better person.

Here are a few things I learned from pouring concrete that can help you in YOUR life, with whatever job YOU have.

- You have to finish what you start - EVERY day.
- You can't just take a break, quit, or go home because you're tired, upset, or hurt. It doesn't matter if it's too cold, too hot, too wet or too dry. You have to finish your job.
- You have to work with others. By yourself, you can't get much done.
- When you're pouring concrete - age, race, culture, or money don't matter. There's only ONE question: Can you get the job done?
- You'll be a better boss if you never ask a worker to do something that you haven't done yourself.

• Working hard makes you appreciate life more, and can give you everything you want in life.

MOST of all, I learned that LIFE IS WHAT YOU MAKE IT.

You can be a simple person and still have a great life.

LAZY

Loafer

Idle

Bum

Shiftless

Lethargic

Do-nothing...

Chapter FIFTEEN

HAVING A WORK ETHIC

"I'm VERY prejudiced.
I HATE lazy people."

Here's a test to see if you're one of them.

Situation:

You just had a load of firewood dumped in your driveway that needs to be carried into your backyard.

- The First Kind of People walk back and forth talking to you while YOU carry the firewood.
- The Second Kind of People pick up wood and help carry it WHILE they talk to you.

Always be the Second Kind of people - the hard-working kind.

Our country has gotten incredibly lazy. It's to the point where no one even wants to work anymore. You can help change that.

Chapter SIXTEEN

HOW DO YOU HAVE A SUCCESSFUL LIFE?

Surround yourself with Good and Not Evil.

- Work hard.
- Tell the truth.
- Help others.
- Go outside and smell the roses.
- Eat a candy bar.
- Tell someone you love them.
- Keep life simple and fun.

If you do these things, you will have a successful life.

HAVING A BAD TEMPER

Chapter SEVENTEEN

At one time, losing your temper worked... but not now.

It used to be that when everything else failed, you could get mad and go nuts...and it got the desired results.

But in today's world, the results you get are that you could be seriously hurt or killed. Everybody's got a gun or a knife.

They don't let the police do their job. Crime today is so far out of control that temper doesn't work.

The best way to deal with your temper today, is to just disassociate yourself from people who make you mad. You have to be smart enough to curb your temper because it can get you killed.

It ALL gets back to drugs.

MARRIAGE

Chapter EIGHTEEN

I had 39 years of great marriage, and we fought and argued every day.

The key ingredients to a successful marriage are True Love and Trust. If you have True Love, no matter how much you fight and argue, you will overcome any problem and stay together. The second key ingredient is Trust, which is a part of True Love.

Living together permanently with another person, without marrying them, is a mistake. It doesn't work. The REASON it doesn't work is because God's laws say it's WRONG.

We have government laws for everything you can think of, and we follow THEM; but more and more, people think God's laws don't matter.

They're wrong.

SEXUALITY OF ALL KINDS

Chapter NINETEEN

Don't flaunt it.

No matter WHAT your lifestyle is, it should be more about love than sex. If the biggest thing in your life is sex... you've been listening to the devil.

It's what you act like toward others that matters. Be unselfish. Be a good friend. The sex-thing has a way of working itself out if you don't make a big deal out of it.

Chapter TWENTY

HOW A PRESIDENT COULD SOLVE OUR PROBLEMS

Listen to the REAL people - NOT the politicians.

Take all the big world problems and talk to the people involved in them. Police problems? Talk to the cops.

Homeless problems? Stop pampering them and make them obey the laws. Get the homeless on committees, and make THEM figure out a solution.

You get the idea.

RELIGIONS

Chapter TWENTY-ONE

I like any form of religion that teaches faith in God.

I was raised a Catholic and that's what works for me. If you look around, you'll find a religion that works for you. Religion gives you rules to live by and something to believe in.

It's a very important part of life.

POLITICS

Chapter TWENTY-TWO

Politics should be
flushed down the drain.

Politics doesn't work. It's a rich man's ploy to put money in his pocket, and it solves nothing.

Trump was an excellent example of what CAN work in politics. He wasn't a politician; he was a businessman... and he did great!

Some people didn't like him because he showed them what they were NOT doing.

Chapter TWENTY-THREE

TEACHERS and EDUCATION

The people who teach our kids should be treated like gold.

We should give teachers the best of the best because they're shaping our children's futures.

Our public schools need to be more structured and disciplined, and teach the kids something. In public school you have to deal with everybody. It's the real world.

Private schools are not the real world; that's why they call it "private." Parents who can afford it, send their kids to private schools because they want more structure for their kids. The believe their kids will be more protected and they will learn more. It's true.

Private schools are becoming more and more popular. Public schools are getting worse and worse. Something has to change, because there are not enough private schools for everybody.

DON'T sit on your ass!"

Chapter TWENTY-FOUR

GROWN-UP CHILDREN WHO DON'T WORK AND STILL LIVE WITH THEIR PARENTS

It's the parents' fault!

This situation seems to be happening more and more, and doesn't help anyone. It keeps grown-up children from having productive lives. It makes parents worry about what will happen to their kids when they're gone.

This situation only happens because parents fail to tell their kids the magic words:

"Get out of here and go get a fuckin' job."

BELIEVE IN MIRACLES

Chapter TWENTY-FIVE

HOW DO YOU KNOW THERE IS A GOD?

I know there's a God because of all the "mini-miracles" I see every day.

A mini-miracle is God showing you He's right here. There are countless mini-miracles every day of our lives, if we just look for them and accept them.

Just look at a tree, a blade of grass, a bird or a deer, a new baby, or a beautiful day. I call these things "mini-miracles." Did MAN make these things? No.

They come from God, just like we do. When we're NOT noticing or appreciating these mini-miracles...we're too full of ourselves.

"When you pray you don't ask. You put yourself in the hands of God."

(Mother Teresa)

Chapter TWENTY-SIX

PRAYING

Pray to God ALL the time.

Ask Him for help and say "Thank you."
I always say "thank you." Praying is like pay-
ing an insurance policy premium to God.

You remember HIM every day - and in
turn, YOU get protection and all these wonderful mini-miracles (and some HUGE mira-
cles) back from Him.

"If there's just ONE thing I wish the
whole world could understand, it would be
the power of prayer."

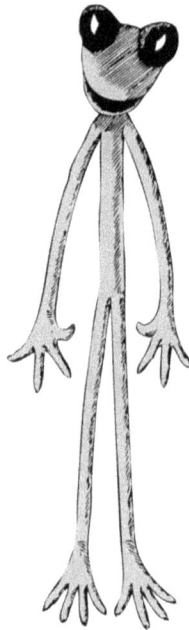

DIETING

Chapter TWENTY-SEVEN

DIETING TOO MUCH

I've never met a person who was super skinny - on purpose - who was smart.

You have to eat to get oxygen to your brain so you can think. Vegetarians get sick more frequently than regular people.

Keeping yourself from getting too fat is more about exercise than food. Everybody in the world should exercise 30 minutes a day, 5 days a week.

ΑΩ

Chapter TWENTY-EIGHT

DEALING WITH LIFE'S BEST AND WORST THINGS

Jesus promised us two things in the Bible.

- **That we would DEFINITELY have problems in our lives.**
- **That if we follow him and pray to God, He will ALWAYS help us overcome them.**

I've had so many wonderful things in my life, including:

- My wife Natalie,
- My deceased wife Suzanne,
- The birth of my son,
- My health.

I've also had some terrible things happen in my life.

- My wife died.
- My son left me.

Through ALL of these things, I never stopped praying, never gave up, and I proved that Jesus was not lying. God got me through ALL my terrible problems, and continues to bless me with wonderful things.

He's waiting to do the same thing for you.

Chapter TWENTY-NINE

FIXING MISTAKES WE'VE MADE

Own up to them and change how you're living your life.

When you have to pay for your OWN sins - and I have certainly paid for mine - you stop doing them.

People (like parents) who try to fix up your mistakes FOR you, are NOT helping you. They're just guaranteeing that you're going to continue to screw up.

"Keep yourself surrounded by true friends"

Chapter THIRTY

MAKING AND KEEPING GOOD FRIENDS

The secret of friendship is finding the right friends.

Find the ones that are true. Find the ones that will be there when you're down. The most important way to make and keep good friends is LOYALTY.

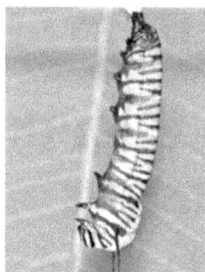

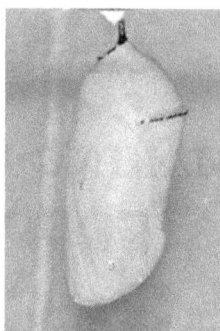

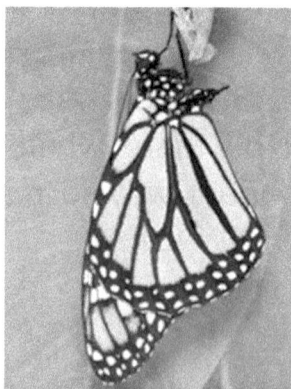

Chapter THIRTY-ONE

DEALING WITH DEATH & WHAT HEAVEN IS LIKE

If you've got faith, you don't have to worry about death.

When it comes, it will be easy. This isn't heaven here, but I want to go there. God is watching and judging us every day to see if we belong in heaven.

I think heaven will be unbelievable - absolutely GREAT! I'll be reunited with all my family... (and my sciatica won't bother me).

Summum

bonum

Chapter THIRTY TWO

THE GREATEST THING A PERSON CAN ACCOMPLISH IN LIFE

To be known as a good, honest, and decent person (who doesn't take drugs).

Life IS tough...but you, too, can conquer it.

Never forget that.

Never forget about God.

"It is better to spend one DAY as a lion, than one hundred YEARS as a lamb."

About the Author

John Peretto is a lifelong resident of Northern California, and a 45-year member of Plasterers' and Cement Masons' Union Local 400 in Vallejo.

He likes spending time with his large extended family and friends, and enjoys cruising estate sales, good cigars, bocce ball, and the annual Columbus Day Parade.

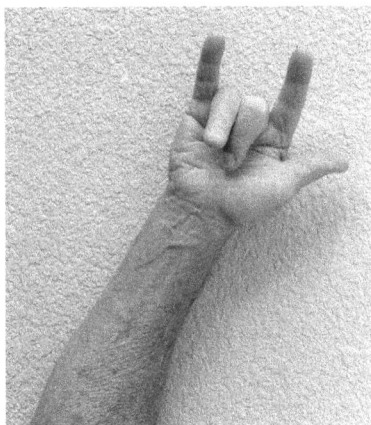

Ascoltami!

www.ingramcontent.com/pod-product-compliance
Lightning Source LLC
Chambersburg PA
CBHW060254030426
42335CB00014B/1693

* 9 7 8 1 9 3 8 8 1 4 6 7 9 *